PASSPORT
RUSSIA

DATE DUE

Passport To The World

Passport Argentina
Passport Brazil
Passport China
Passport France
Passport Germany
Passport Hong Kong
Passport India
Passport Indonesia
Passport Israel
Passport Italy
Passport Japan
Passport Korea
Passport Malaysia
Passport Mexico
Passport Philippines
Passport Poland
Passport Singapore
Passport South Africa
Passport Spain
Passport Taiwan
Passport Thailand
Passport United Kingdom
Passport USA
Passport Vietnam

PASSPORT RUSSIA

Your Pocket Guide to Russian Business, Customs & Etiquette

Charles Mitchell

Passport Series Editor: Barbara Szerlip

WORLD TRADE PRESS®
Professional Books for International Trade

"Passport to the World" concept: Edward G. Hinkelman
Cover design: Peter Jones, Marge Wilhite
Illustrations: Tom Watson
Desktop publishing: Joe Reif

This publication is designed to provide general information con-
cerning the cultural aspects of doing business with people from a
particular country. It is sold with the understanding that the pub-
lisher is not engaged in rendering legal or any other professional
services. If legal advice or other expert assistance is required, the
services of a competent professional person should be sought.

Mitchell, Charles, 1953–
Passport Russia: your pocket guide to Russian business,
customs & etiquette / Charles Mitchell.
p. cm. -- (Passport to the world)
Includes bibliographical references.
ISBN 1-885073-32-1
1. Corporate culture -- Russia (Federation) 2. Business etiquette -- Russia (Federation) 3. Negotiation in business --
Russia (Federation) 4. Intercultural communication. I. Title.
II. Series.
HD58.7.M564 1998
390' .00947--dc21
97-45163 CIP

Printed in the United States of America

Table of Contents

RUSSIA

Coping with Capitalism

Overview

Business Environment

Customs & Etiquette

Additional Information

RUSSIA
Quick Look

Official name	Russian Federation
Land area	6,592,800 sq mi (17,075,400 sq km)
Highest elevation	Mt. Klyuchhevskaya 15,812 ft (14,458 m)
Lowest elevation	Caspian Sea 62 ft (18.9 m)
Capital & largest city	Moscow, 8.8 million

People
Population (1996)   148,178,487
Distribution   73% urban, 27% rural
Annual Growth   0.07%
Official Language   Russian
Major religions   Russian Orthodox, Islam, Protestantism, Judaism

Economy
GDP (1996)   US$796 billion
US$5,300 per capita
Foreign Trade (1996)   Imports US$57.9 billion
Exports US$77.8 billion
Surplus US$19.3 billion
Currency (12/97)   1Ruble (R) = 100 Kopecks
Ruble 5,971 = US$1*

Education and health
Literacy (1996)   98%
Physicians   1 per 226 persons
Life Expectancy   Men 56.5 years
Women 70.3 years

*Note: The government plans to lop three zeros off the value in January 1998: thus in new rubles, 5.9 rubles =$1

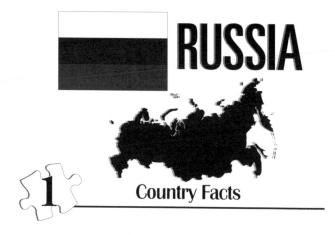

RUSSIA

1 Country Facts

Geography & Demographics

Russia is the largest country on the planet, covering one-eighth of the earth's surface and stretching across 11 time zones from Europe to Asia. It shares borders with Finland, Poland, Norway, Estonia, Latvia, Lithuania, Belarus, Ukraine and Turkey in the north and west, as well as Georgia, Azerbaijan, Kazakstan, North Korea, Mongolia and China in the south and east. The country's three major rivers west of the Urals (a mountain range that separates Russia's European and Asian regions) all originate within 400 kilometers of Moscow and flow south to the Caspian and Black Seas.

Most of Russia is covered by vast barren plains, but it's also home to dramatic tundras in the Arctic north, forests, steppes, the black earth belt (some of the world's richest soil) and semidesert.

Russia is the sixth-most-populated nation in the world (after China, India, the U.S., Indonesia and Brazil) and its largest cities have populations exceeding those of some European countries. It's inhabited by 130 different ethnic and language groups, including Russians (81 percent), Tartars, Ukrainians, Belarussians, Yakuts, Bashkirs and Chuvashs. An additional 25 million Russians live beyond the country's borders, mostly in neighboring states of the former U.S.S.R.

Mineral Rich

The country is rich in natural resources, though many reserves are considered almost inaccessible due to poor infrastructure and the extreme climate. Russia produces as much as 30 percent of the world's nonferrous, rare, and noble metals, 17 percent of the world's crude oil, 30 percent of its natural gas, and it holds 40 percent of the world's known natural gas reserves (mostly in Siberia). It's also one of the largest gold producers on earth. It has more than one-fifth of the world's forested land and more than half of its standing coniferous timber.

Climate

Moscow lies on the same latitude as the lower portion of Canada's Hudson Bay. The average summer temperature in Moscow and St. Petersburg is about 24°C (75°F). But it is the long and dark winter (Moscow experiences about five hours of daylight at the height of winter) that defines the country. The Moscow River generally freezes by mid-November, with snow remaining until the April thaw. The average January temperature in Moscow is -12°C (10°F). The city of Vladivostock in the far east has an average winter temperature of -13°C (9°F). While Siberia is thought of as a frozen wasteland — winter temperatures range between -20°C and -36°C (-4°F to -33°F) — it gets positively balmy in summer, with many areas reaching 16°C (61°F). The coldest inhabited settlement on earth is Russia's Omyakon in the far northeast, where the average winter temperature is a crisp -67°C (Celsius and Fahrenheit cross at -40°).

Business Hours

Despite Russia's size, office and shopping hours are fairly consistent in major urban areas. Business offices open between 8 and 9 A.M. and close by 5 or 5:30 P.M. Monday through Friday. (Moscow and St. Petersburg are three hours ahead of Greenwich Mean Time and eight hours ahead of U.S. Eastern Standard Time.) A few businesses close for lunch (generally between 1 and 2 P.M.) but most remain open, even if only manned by a less-than-helpful skeleton staff. Management lunches often last two to three hours, so be forewarned about lateness after the lunch break. Russian employees are notorious clock watchers and working overtime is rare. Many offices have regularly scheduled Saturday morning hours, though these are almost never used for meeting with foreign visitors.

Banks generally open at 8 A.M. and close by 2 or 3 P.M. Monday through Friday. Shops are open from 9 A.M. to 6 P.M. Monday through Saturday; some are beginning to keep longer hours until 8 P.M. Many, however, do close early on Saturdays. As a general rule, late-night shopping doesn't exist.

Regarding religious holidays, be aware that the Russian Orthodox Church follows the Julian calendar, which generally runs about thirteen days behind the Gregorian one used throughout the Western world.

National Holidays

January 1: New Year's Day
> Akin to the western Christmas Day (see Chapter 16: Customs).

January 7: Eastern Orthodox Christmas
> The Christian answer to New Year's Day.

March 8: International Woman's Day
> Celebrates the female contribution to world culture.

April 1: Day of the Foundation of the Commonwealth of Russia and Belarussia
> Marks the formal union between Russia and Belarussia. Many Russians want little to do with taking on a sick neighbor.

May 1: May Day, or International Labor Day
> Formerly celebrated with elaborate parades. Today, it's mostly thought of as a day off for blue-collar workers.

May 9: Victory Day
> Marks the end of World War II and the defeat of Nazi Germany. It also gives rise to nostalgic memories of how great the Soviet Union once was and to calls from the Fascist fringe to rehabilitate Joseph Stalin.

June 12: Declaration of Independence
> Marks the formal breakup of the Soviet Union and the end of Communism.

November 7: November Revolution
> Once the country's most important holiday, it marks the coming to power of the Communists during the 1917 Bolshevik Revolution. While still marked by a scaled-down military parade and marches, it has lost much of its luster.

December 12: Constitution Day
> Celebrates the new constitution of Russia that replaced the Soviet one.

Although not official national holidays, much of the country observes Good Friday and Easter Monday (dates vary), as well as All Saints' Day (November 1) and Christmas Day (December 25).

2   The Russians

I cannot forecast to you the action of Russia. It is a riddle wrapped in a mystery inside an enigma.
Sir Winston Churchill, Oct. 1, 1939

A Preference for Order

Churchill's famous words were never more apt than they are today. At least under Communism, Russians knew their role and likely opportunities. Though most were not very well off financially, they tended to be comfortable with the social order. Today, the "you eat what you kill" attitude of the new market economy, coupled with a prevalent Frontier Mentality ("anything goes, especially when it comes to money and sex") are contrary to the traditional Russian character.

Since ancient times, Russians have always preferred order over chaos, at the cost of freedom. The Russian Primary Chronicles (a comprehensive history compiled in the early 12th century) describes how Slavic tribes inhabiting Russia around 860 A.D. petitioned three Scandinavian lords — Ryurik, Sineus and Truvor — to rule over them, pleading, "Our whole land is great and rich but there is no order in it."

The three obliged, and Russians have almost always had strong (if somewhat ruthless) leaders since — ranging from Ivan the Terrible (1533-1584), who earned his title after ordering the slaughter of thousands of suspected coup plotters; to Peter the Great (1682-1725), who opened Russia to the West (and incidentally had the heads of more than 100 coup plotters displayed on stakes throughout St. Petersburg); to Catherine the Great (1762-1796), a great reformer who nonetheless suppressed a two-year peasant revolt; to Joseph Stalin (1924-1953), who historians now credit with facilitating the deaths of somewhere between 20 and 25 million innocents.

Not Sure Who They Are Anymore

More than 80 years ago, rallying under the image of a hammer and sickle (symbol of the forced marriage of worker and peasant), Lenin and his Bolshevik Revolution brought an end to three centuries of rule by imperial Romanov Tsars. Then, in 1991, within a matter of months, Lenin's Soviet Union, a.k.a. the U.S.S.R., vanished. Today, less than a decade since the collapse of Communist rule, the Russians are a confused lot.

The confusion really began with Mikhail Gorbachev's terrible twins: *glasnost* (openness) and *perestroika* (restructuring) in the mid-1980s. Meant to make corrupt Soviet officials more accountable by increasing the flow of information through mass media, the limited freedoms these policies granted quickly spun out of control. (They also backfired. Previously, local disasters weren't reported in the Soviet media. But under *glasnost*, the press was suddenly filled with reports of train derailments, airplane crashes, droughts and the like, giving the impression that under Gorbachev, the country had gone to hell in a handbasket.)

Confusion also stems from the fact that what were previously crimes (economic speculation, private ownership of property) are now virtues and that the ability to think and act independently — traits that once led to long stays in Siberian *gulags* (Stalin's "correctional" labor camps) — is now the essence of success, if not survival. Also, the current transition from Communism to Capitalism is being played out against the backdrop of the largest privatization of a national economy in the history of the world (a process that many believe was "fixed" from the start). To say that the Russians are in the midst of a national identity crisis is an understatement.

Language: Not As Hard As It Looks

The Cyrillic alphabet (reputedly invented by St. Cyril circa 863 A.D.) is well organized around phonetics, and Russian words are pronounced as they're spelled (unlike English words). A few hours spent familiarizing yourself with the alphabet will debunk much of its mystery.

Some paranoia about maintaining the language's purity is beginning to creep in. Moscow shop signs are now required to be in Russian, after a spate of English-language signs threatened to turn some shopping districts into mini-American malls. Slang (both Russian and English) is also making an appearance after decades of having been banned from printed media.

Under Communism, Russian was mandatory in schools and media and encouraged in government and business throughout the Soviet Union's many republics. This attempt by Moscow to "Russify" its Soviet states (within which more than 100 different languages were spoken) led non-Russians to view the language as a tool of the oppressor.

While Russians may appreciate your attempts to use the language (and it's easy to speak it poorly), doing so in places like the Ukraine or Georgia is likely to earn you a rebuke or at least a cold stare.

The Incredible Shrinking Country

Uncertainty about the future and the unevenness of the market economy — resulting in a greater number of Russians being worse off economically than during the Soviet era — has left Russia relatively childless. Since the late 1980s, the birth rate has fallen below replacement level. Abortion, the most common form of birth control, outnumbers live births by more than a two-to-one margin. The procedure was legalized here in 1920; today, having eight or nine in a lifetime isn't unheard of.

Under the Soviet regime, motherhood was a much-valued weapon of the empire. (After all, the more territory you controlled, the more Russians you needed to rule it.) Gone is the enticement of awarding special economic and social privileges to the prolific, who could earn the title of "Heroine Mother – Second Class" for providing the empire with five children. (First Class was reserved for women who brought ten or more little Soviets into the world.)

The end of state interference in bedroom affairs, along with poor public health and education, has made child bearing and rearing a luxury. (The number of abandoned and homeless kids has exploded.) Due to a chronic housing shortage in major cities, another luxury is privacy. (Coincidentally, there's no word in the Russian language for "privacy.") Apartments here often consist of only one or two rooms, with the living room doubling as the bedroom. Some Russians actually cover over the eyes of their religious icons when they're planning to have sex in the same room with them — a habit encouraged by Russian Orthodox priests.

Alcoholism: A National Pastime?

More Russians are drowned in a bottle of vodka than people in all the oceans of the world goes an ancient proverb. The ability to consume (or at least attempt to consume) great quantities of alcohol (usually vodka) in short periods is still considered a measure of manhood here, and of womanhood to a lesser extent. As a result, an estimated 10 percent of the population suffers from alcoholism, one-third of all violent crimes are alcohol-related, and national life expectancy rates are declining.

Back in the 10th century, Grand Prince Vladimir I embraced Christianity rather than Islam, knowing that his subjects would never accept a religion that banned alcohol. During the mid 1980s, Soviet leader Mikhail Gorbachev — himself a teetotaler and thus, in Russian conventional wisdom, not someone to be trusted wholeheartedly — ordered a cutback on national vodka production and drastically reduced selling hours. The result? The country's treasury lost approximately 20 percent of its tax revenue and the nation experienced a severe sugar shortage, as Russians took to setting up stills and making their own brews (known as *samogon*). Today, per capita consumption of hard liquor in Russia's major cities is the highest in the world — more than 50 liters annually.

(For more on vodka, see Chapter 19: Entertaining.)

Violence: All In The Family

Russian "family values" have never been lower.

During the Soviet era, with its system based on nepotism and connections, a strong and loyal extended family was a survival trick. It's not that the Soviets encouraged strong family structure; loyalty to the State was the priority. (One of the official heroes of the Communist youth movement was Pavlik Morosov, a young tike who, during Stalin's reign, denounced his father as a traitor for hoarding grain. His father was executed and Pavlik was subsequently murdered by revengeful uncles.) In the end, though, family members were considered among the few individuals one could at least half-way trust. But the "me first" attitude of the new Russia is reflected in the near-total collapse of what's left of that traditional structure.

Alcoholism, unemployment and the pressures of adapting to a new way of life have led to an epidemic of family violence and spousal abuse. Many Russians (not least of all civil servants and police) still pay homage to such folk wisdom as, "If he beats you, that means he loves you." The government estimates that between 20 and 30 percent of the country's murder victims are members of the killer's immediate family. Russian men tend to view their families as private possessions, to be done with as they please.

Nasha Luchshe: Ours is Best

"Russia is not at all like Poland," goes another proverb, "Russia has bigger people." That sums up how the Russians view themselves — as bigger, better and smarter than most other nationalities. Decades spent as the world's "other superpower" re-enforced centuries of superior attitude — one that the cold light of the information age has exposed as having little basis in fact. Still, the belief that Russia remains a great nation, a player on the world stage, is very much part of the national character.

The Russian people have survived Mongol invasions (13th century), Napoleon and his troops at the gates of Moscow (1812), Nazis occupying great swaths of their country (1941-1945), and the social and economic depravations of Communism. This hurtful, initial phase of Capitalism — the "robber baron phase," as many call it — will also pass. It's just another time when the Russian capacity for stoicism comes in handy. Beneath this outward appearance of hard times lies something that was mostly lacking during the last 80 years — an underpinning of hope. One Russian school teacher who survives on handouts puts it this way: "Years ago, I had what I needed, regular pay, money to pay for clothes and food, respect from my neighbors. Now I have none of that, but at least my children will have a chance to do better, to become rich. Before, there was no future. Now, anything can happen if they work hard."

Commerce Da, Intellectualism Nyet

Entrepreneurs and bankers are the new elite, replacing the coddled and heavily subsidized intellectuals, the "haves" of the Soviet era (now elliptically referred to as *ranshe* — "earlier"). The scientist, the professor and the writer once led charmed lives, privy to imported goods, summer *dachas* (country houses) and high respect. Today, they're near the bottom of the social heap.

Due to privatization and severe budget cuts, a science "brain drain" has occurred, with many of the country's finest theoretical physicists, nuclear engineers and mathematicians fleeing, often to well-financed U.S. laboratories and universities.

The average Russian reads three times as many books per year as the average American, but despite a proud literary heritage, reading habits have changed. Pop psychology, sexual technique, astrology, murder mysteries, and clever titles like *KGB Guidebook to the Cities of the World* (a collaboration by seven ex-secret service agents, laced with spy lore and undercover travel tips) are now the preferred fare. Part of the problem is that there are few reviewers or large bookstores to create a momentum. Most books are sold in street stalls, which specialize in lurid covers that catch the eyes of busy pedestrians.

"Could Tolstoy or Chekhov survive in this era?" asks a Russian author and university professor who flourished under the old regime. "I doubt it. They would be out selling comic books or writing advertising scripts. You have to wonder how many good authors and artists will be lost to commercialism. This is the hidden price of our new order."

Age: The Great Divide

While age once had its privileges in Russia (World War II veterans got to go to the head of the bread queue, for example), youth is the valued commodity today. The generation that the Communists once feared as being lost has been found — counting its money.

An inordinate amount of the new and still emerging Russian middle class (those with decent paying jobs, mostly with foreign firms) are under the age of 40. They simply don't have the political baggage or the Communist-era work ethic of their parent's and grandparent's generations.

The Church Revival

Even during the officially aetheist Communist era, when the cult of Lenin ("the red tsar") reigned, millions remained secretly loyal to the Russian Orthodox Church. Though the Soviet constitution guaranteed religious freedom, the Church was, in reality, just another Party-controlled organization, with many of its senior officers and priests appointed only with the government's approval. Like puppets, they would be trotted out at times of national crisis to serve as a unifying force.

Today, this thousand-year-old institution is back with a vengeance, having been incorporated into many state ceremonial functions by President Boris Yeltsin. The Church runs homeless shelters, food banks and orphanages, and several foreign aid agencies use it as a conduit to ensure that the needy receive help. Church endorsement provides businessmen, politicians and sometimes even Communists with a cultural and patriotic stamp of approval. Stolichny Savings, one of the country's biggest banks, donated 50 kilograms of gold to adorn Moscow's cathedral dome. Very protective of its newly found status, the Russian Orthodox Church is seeking a law that would ban most other religions from the country.

Nothing Foreign About Foreigners Anymore

The novelty of the foreigner has worn off. Familiarity has bred contempt. By and large, the Russians are tired of the flood of advisors, scam artists and get-rich-quick schemers that has swept through their borders in recent years. Today, Russians tend to view them as access to capital, targets for muggings, and generally as people from whom a skilled or clever Russian can make money.

While Americans — with their arrogance and "do it our way" attitude — haven't particularly endeared themselves, Russians still harbor a grudging respect, believing that only they and the Americans are the superpowers that count. As for Europeans, the Russians still feel vastly superior to them. Asian businesspeople (with the exception of the Chinese) are treated with great respect in the Russian far east, but the further west they move, the less they're liked or respected.

Pride in Achievement

Russia's pre-Soviet contributors to world literature include Alexander Pushkin (*Yvegeny Onegin*), N.V. Gogol (*The Government Inspector*) Fedor Dostovevsky (*The Brothers Karamazov*), Leo Tolstoy (*War and Peace, Anna Karenina*), and Anton Chekhov (*The Cherry Orchard, Uncle Vanya*). More contemporary writers — Boris Pasternak, Mikhail Bulgakov, Aleksander Solzhenitsyn — have continued the tradition, often at great personal cost. Its performing arts legacy includes composers Dimitry Shostakovich, Modest Petrovich Mussorgsky and Petor Tchaikovsky, and the ballet dancers Anna Pavlova, Rudolph Nureyev and Mikhail Baryshnikov.

Forgotten by (or unknown to) many is that between the 1890s and 1917, Russia was at the forefront of Modernism; painters like Alexander Rodchenko and Kasimir Malevich helped set the tone for the 1920s avant-garde movement in Paris. Filmmaker Sergie Eisenstein (*Battleship Potemkin*, 1926; *The Strike*, 1925) has been hailed as an innovator in the mold of Alfred Hitchcock and Andrei Tarkovsky (*The Mirror, The Stalker Nostalgia)* as a cinematic genius. More recently, Nikita Mikalhov's *Burnt by the Sun* won a Hollywood Oscar.

In 1905, Ivan Pavlov won the Nobel Prize for his famous study of conditioned reflexes in dogs. And although the Soviets ultimately lost the race to first land a man on the moon, they launched the first satellite into space (Sputnik, 1957), the first man in space (Yuri Gagarin, 1961), the first woman in space (Valentina Tereshkova, 1963), the first

unmanned lunar landing (Luna 9, 1966), and the
first permanently manned space station, the Mir.

We Invented It

Still, an underlying feeling of inferiority has led
to some rather odd and exaggerated claims. Official
Russian encyclopedias cite Alexander Lodygin (not
Thomas Edison) as the inventor of the electric light
bulb. They also state that Alexander Mozhaisky
was a decade ahead of the Wright Brothers in making the first airplane and that Alexander Popov (not
Guglielmo Marconi) invented the radio. One American journalist, writing a story about the burgeoning Russian interest in baseball in the mid-1980s,
was informed in all sincerity by a government
sports official that baseball had, in fact, been
invented by the Russians more than a century
before the Americans ever even dreamed of it;
indeed, the American "version" was a weak deriva-
tive of the Russian game of *lapda*.

In the spirit of such pride, few Russians will
admit to the origin of Russia's white, blue and red
national flag. It seems that the flag was designed by
Peter the Great (1672–1725) who, impressed by the
work ethic and technical acumen of the citizens of
Holland, simply rearranged the Dutch flag's hori-
zontal stripes.

3 Cultural Stereotypes

The Cold War image of Russians as dour, unhealthy, overweight, poorly dressed, deeply brooding alcoholics willing to queue for hours for toilet paper while waiting for their leadership to dominate the world has faded as the country opens to new ideas and global contacts. However, new stereotypes are being born as the Russians discover the pains, joys and decadence that wealth and a free market can bring.

Brooding

All Russians are darkly introspective.

True, Russians always stop to analyze why things happen and to discover a deeper meaning within life's most mundane aspects. Moodiness is an essential aspect of the Russian soul, as is an enormous capacity for stoicism and suffering in silence. None of Russia's greatest novels have happy endings; Russians wouldn't know what to make of them if they did.

New Money, Bad Manners

The new Russian wealthy are extremely uncouth.

There's really is no such thing as "old money" in Russia; the Communists saw to that. With the nobility long purged, economic speculation a crime, and foreign travel and information tightly restricted throughout the Soviet era, newly wealthy Russians have no models on which to base their behavior. The more glamorous, wasteful and decadent one can be, the more wealthy one is *perceived* as being. Ordering $500 bottles of champagne — for take out — from Moscow's Maxim's of Paris restaurant is just one example. Gaudy clothes, luxury cars (preferably German Mercedes Benz 600s), bodyguards, cell phones, expensive watches and nonexistent manners are their hallmarks.

In many European coastal resorts, this new elite has replaced Ugly Americans as the popular laughing stock. Typical joke: A "New Russian" boasts that he just spent US$2,000 on a tie at the Gucci store in Moscow. "That's a shame," says his drinking mate. "I know a place where you can get the identical tie for $5,000."

However, fear of attracting the attention of the criminal element and worry over kidnappings, extortion and robberies are forcing a rethink. Also, several publications directed at the new Russian rich offer advise on everything from proper table manners to scheduling the house maid's day off so that it causes the least disruption to the master and mistress's routine.

Corrupt

Business and politics are dominated by crooks.

Public shoot-outs and press coverage of contract murders have fueled this idea. According to the government, 46 Russian businessmen and 4 parliamentarians were assassinated in 1995 and 49 bankers (specifically) in the first eight months of 1996. Few of these crimes were solved, though many have been linked to the Russian Mafia, which has a real presence (see Chapter 13: Business Outside the Law). Also, many of the country's earliest entrepreneurs emerged from the "black market" that thrived during the Leonid Brezhnev era.

Politicians often ignore public opinion, as there are few trade unions or powerful political parties to tie them to the needs of the average Russian. As for the voice of media, many newspapers, magazines and TV stations have been bought up by tycoons with strong government ties. "We have gained freedom, but a strange freedom," observed human rights activist Yelena Bonner (Andrei Sakharov's widow), referring to the state's 1996 war against its own citizens in Chechnya in which as many as 100,000 may have perished. "It is such a freedom that our elected leaders consider themselves absolutely free from the people's control."

Racist

Russians look down on all ethnic minorities, especially those with dark skin.

Unfortunately, this is often true. As rulers of a Soviet empire that once included more than 100 different minority nationalities, the Russians never lost their sense of superiority. Citizens still carry internal passports stamped with their "nationality," be it Russian, Chechen or Jew. Anti-semitism is common.

Police have reportedly beaten up thousands of dark-skinned people from Central Asia and the Caucasus (such as Tartars and Armenians) and thrown them out of Moscow, with the mayor's blessing. Neo-Nazi skinheads have been known to roam the area near Patrice Lumumba University looking for foreign students ("monkeys") to assault. The Japanese are considered inferior. And many Russians will go out of their way to avoid proximity to a black man or woman, even on crowded public transportation, as they believe that blacks carry the AIDS virus and don't want to be near them.

West is Best

Russians have an insatiable appetite for Western goods.

Choice is a fairly new luxury here. Gone are the days when G.U.M., Moscow's largest department store, carried only one style of female bathing attire, leading to the odd sight of a river beach dotted with dozens of the same faux leopardskin bikini. Gone, too, are the days of trading a pair of worn Levi's for caviar and icons. Stores are piled high with everything from Coca Cola, hotdogs and Calvin Klein underwear to IBM computers and imported luxury cars. Advertising, especially on TV, is a new art form here and it fuels the Russian appetite. According to the *Wall Street Journal*, "Even the Communists who decry Western influence do so dressed in Italian suits while trying to woo Western executives in Swiss ski resorts."

4 Regional Differences

Russification

The Russians were empire builders and fairly ruthless colonialists who forced their language and culture down the throats of their conquered neighbors. Moscow-based central control succeeded in building cities that look remarkably similar and in creating a population that, although diverse, thinks and speaks alike — at least on the surface. However, this Russification program backfired with the collapse of the Soviet Union; given the opportunity, countries such as the Baltic Republics, Ukraine and Georgia bolted faster than runaway troikas.

For the most part, regional differences stem more from socioeconomic conditions than from ethnic origin. Now that Moscow is busy with larger issues, several smaller republics, like Tartarstan, enjoy a greater degree of autonomy. The downside of this is that these republics no longer have anyone to blame but themselves for economic shortcomings and local mismanagement.

Moscow As Center Of The Universe

The "boom town" mentality in St. Petersburg and Moscow is about as far removed from the stagnation of the countryside as Earth is from Mars. Despite recent peasant roots, the Russian city dweller isn't fond of his country cousin (and the feeling is mutual). Urban Russians joke about the "revolting peasants" — a revealing double entendre.

Though there's money to burn in Moscow, there's precious little investment to allow for private enterprise in the provinces (where at least 95 percent of farmers still operate in communal fashion), and resentments have mushroomed. Many areas have been crippled by strikes over unpaid government wages. The average wage delay in the government-run coal industry, for example, is more than five months. As a result, migration to the cities has been nothing short of spectacular.

Compounding the divide are the millions of Russians who moved to small mining and timber towns in Siberia and the Ural Mountains with the promise from the Communist government of higher salaries, new cars and an apartment back in Moscow after working a three- or five-year contract. Today, they're trapped in these industrial backwaters, unable to save enough money to move and bitter about having been forgotten.

Siberia

The huge expanse of frozen nothingness whose name means "sleeping land" is responsible for 24 percent of the country's industrial output and as much as half of all hard cash receipts. It's home to the world's largest deposits of natural gas and is a lucrative source of gold, diamonds, furs (sable, mink, fox, reindeer, squirrel), strategic metals and timber. The average Siberian worker produces 58 percent more than the average Russian on the "mainland," and his wages are higher by 30 percent.

But many consider Siberia to be a hellhole. Though much of its four million square miles remains unaffected by human activity, inhabitants of the largest industrial centers — Angarsk, Bratsk, Kemerovo, Krasnoyarsk, Novokuznetsk and Norilsk — live in an ecological nightmare. The air, the water and the soil are all heavily polluted because of 1950s technology and a dearth of pollution-control programs.

The CIS

Created in 1991 and comprised of newly independent countries that once belonged to the Soviet Union, the 12-member Commonwealth of Independent States (CIS) was envisaged by Moscow as a tightly woven confederation controlled by Russia. But it failed successively as a military union, a currency union and as an economic one, with all of the former Soviet republics (with the exception of Belarus) running as fast and as far away as possible.

While CIS members continue to trade heavily with Moscow (mostly for geographic reasons), all are pursuing their own interests — with the Ukraine looking more to the West and Europe than to Russia, and the Muslim republics in the south seeking allies in the Middle East and Turkey. They do get together to talk, but it's usually to do a bit of Russia-bashing. At the same time, they remain wary of Russia's expansionist bent and its capacity for military coercion. In April 1997, for example, Azerbaijan discovered that its neighbor, Armenia, had received an unauthorized US$1 billion worth of arms from the Russian army.

Government & Business

The Great Russian Sell-Off

Prior to 1991, the government owned everything from giant arms factories to retail stores. Today, the sale (some would say give-away) of the century is almost over; more than 120,000 formerly state-owned enterprises have been privatized, including 75 percent of the country's factories and 85 percent of its wholesale and retail trade. (It was, claims *The Economist*, "a ferocious, unregulated affair in which bombs, shotguns and even toxin on teacups seem to have played as big a part as bids, offers and due-diligence searches.") In the process, both new millionaires and a new poverty class were created.

Those whom the government still employs it can't pay; it's in arrears for salaries, wages and pension payments to between 65 and 75 million workers. The Moscow city government was so strapped for cash that it decided to rent out advertising space to private companies on Red Square for May Day celebrations — a move that surely had Lenin turning over in his mausoleum, just across the cobblestones from ads for fax machines and stereos. (The most important Soviet holiday after November Revolution, May Day — the international day of the worker — was really an anti-capitalist celebration.)

Old Communists, New Wealth

Russia is a prime example of the French adage, "The more things change, the more they stay the same." While Russia is full of very young, newly rich entrepreneurs, it also has a huge share of old Communists who cashed in, at rock-bottom prices, on connections and contacts during the aforementioned privatization.

Explains one American sales representative who frequents Moscow: "The new guys get all the ink, but I'll tell you the folks who made a killing are the old Commies who had at least half a brain. These guys bought the factories they were running for a few *rubles* and are making out like bandits."

Veksels: A Novel Approach to IOUs

Russia is currently saddled with US$123 billion worth of unpaid, overdue bills, known here as *veksels*. This has given birth to an unregulated and often informal $15 billion bond market. Some debts are redeemable for cash, others for commodities like tires, cement, electricity or natural gas. According to the *New York Times*, Russian banks and brokerage companies are trading more than US$100 million worth of *veksels* every month, with prices posted on the Internet. The profits are said to be significantly higher than those earned by conventional government bonds — in some cases, as high as 65 percent.

Taxing Times

Ask foreign businesspeople what their biggest headache is in the new Russia and the inevitable answer (after crime) is taxes. Though the top corporate rate is, on average, only 32 percent, it's not unknown for small businesses to be charged more than 100 percent of their profits. The tax laws are a Marx Brothers comedy (Groucho, Harpo and Zippo, not Karl); there are currently in excess of 1,000 different laws on the books. Some conflict, others seem to change daily. Many companies and individuals avoid paying taxes altogether, a potential revenue that may be equivalent to as much as 50 percent of Russia's gross domestic product.

"I could bring in two tax accountants and let them do the books, and I would get figures that wouldn't come close to matching," says one European business manager. "The tax you pay one month is gone, raised, lowered or superseded the next. They just don't get it yet. Even if I *wanted* to pay taxes, I couldn't get anyone to tell me what I owe."

Yet despite its desperate need for foreign investment, the government has *increased* trade barriers by raising tariffs and slapping a 20 percent value-added tax on many imports. Such zigzagging is playing havoc with foreign investors eager to cash in on one of the last great untapped consumer frontiers. It's hoped that the government will initiate major tax reforms sooner rather than later.

Unofficial Taxes

While the government has dumped most of its assets (expect in the highly lucrative natural resources sector), government officials haven't quite relinquished themselves to the sidelines.

"Every time I turn around, there's a bureaucrat

at the door, saying this paper has expired or this law has changed and that I need a new permit," complains one American restaurant owner. "I can deal with the big issues, but the day-to-day reality is that these government guys have their hands out all the time — and for big money."

The biggest barrier to commerce is the lack of enforceable business laws. Deals rely on handshakes and sometimes on the threat of retaliation, but there's no legal recourse. Adds the restaurant owner, "This is high risk, high reward. The people who do well here have a real gunslinger mentality."

Trouble Ahead?

Few would argue that Russia might reverse its present course toward a market economy. Among other encouraging signs:

- Inflation has dropped from an astronomical 2,505 percent in 1992 to 15 percent in 1997
- The Russian stock market, while highly volatile, has achieved some remarkable returns in the 1990s
- One in two Russian families own their own home (part of the privatization "give away"), and 62 percent own land (forbidden under Soviet law and still an issue).

But unreformed Communists (who still hold the largest single bloc in the Duma, the lower house of parliament) have made enough noise to worry some foreign investors. "Could they turn this thing around and stop it?" asks one American company officer. "No, not now. They could make things rougher than they are, but the train has left the station — and it isn't coming back."

6 The Work Environment

The Work Ethic: Is There One?

Because Russians have been living under authoritarian and autocratic rule for more than a millennium, they have no institutional memory of free markets (unlike other recently "freed" Communist nations like Poland, Hungary and East Germany). Communism crushed private initiative and incentive; the social contract between the Soviet state and its workers was, "I pretend to work and you pretend to pay me." The value (or, perhaps more accurately, the rewards) of hard work was relatively unknown here until very recently.

Deadlines were unimportant (and mostly unenforceable) and the pace of work was uneven at best — weeks of inactivity followed by a frenzied week of meeting quotas and targets. Everyone was employed by the state or a state enterprise, and Russians would boast how they could go for days without actually putting in an appearance. They simply left their jackets draped over their chairs and teacups on their desks to make it look like they were somewhere in the building. The Russian verb *sidyet* (to sit) was sometimes used to describe the perfect job in the Soviet bureaucracy. Those days are, of course, history.

Experience May Work Against You

So ingrained was the superior, uncaring attitude in the retail and service sectors that when large foreign hotel chains began opening their doors in Moscow, those seeking employment who had had previous experience in the industry under Soviet rule were automatically disqualified.

"Soviet hotels were like a cross between a prison and a strict private school dormitory," recalls a European who travels frequently to Russia. "These scowly faced *babushkas* [old women] would roam the halls, putting their noses in everyone's business. [Known as the *dejurynayia*, these terrors of the tourist were assigned to report on every foreigner's activities.] It was like coming home to mother. Nowadays, the better hotels are like any others you'll find in Europe. The staff are helpful, pleasant and hard working. They're also young."

Not So Different, After All

With most of the economy now privatized, Russia has a basic mix of every business type, from small, family-run units and street peddlers to midsized professional firms and massive "private enterprises" (formerly state-run behemoths, mostly in heavy manufacturing). In the latter case, many "old style" factory managers have shown themselves to be out of their depth in the new market economy. The smaller and newer the firm, the more likely that it's being run by "new" (if somewhat inexperienced) management.

"A few years ago, Russians would tell me that this country is unique and that it would never be able to conduct business the way it's done in the rest of the world," recalls an American corporate consultant who has been working with Russian businesses for years. "They would say, 'Russia has its own pace and way of doing things.' But guess what? They're finally coming to the conclusion that if the laws of gravity apply universally, so do the basic laws of Capitalism and market economies. Business structures here are beginning to look more and more like they do anywhere else in the world."

While more and more Russians are developing work habits similar to those of their American and European counterparts, it's still rare to find Russians who start their work day before 9 A.M. or end after 6 P.M., and more often than not, lunch lasts a couple of hours.

Status in the Workplace

The rigidity of the Communist-era workplace has given way to more flexibility, though many Russians remain reluctant to seek out responsibility and contribute ideas. Nonetheless, many businesses are beginning to resemble meritocracies.

Many older Russians still associate making money in business with Soviet-era speculation and profiteering. To them, as well as to a large number of the now-dispossessed "intelligencia," business is dirty and without dignity.

More and more, status is being defined by an employee's or partner's ability to bring in new business and less and less by seniority or education (unless that education involved an overseas business management school). Among lower level and emerging middle-class Russians, *who* you work for counts more than what you actually *do*. Employment by a foreign company is considered highly prestigious. On a management level, the more foreign contacts a Russian has, the higher his or her status is likely to be.

Decision Making

Russia's old-command economy left decision making up to a small cadre of high-ranking individuals within each firm or ministry, and it was understood that decisions made in line with Party policy couldn't be wrong. Today, despite the changes, decision making remains an excruciatingly slow process, as most major ones are made by committee and consensus. Responsibility has been slow to filter down to the rank and file, and besides, many employees simply don't want it.

Hamburger Flippers with M.D.s

With much government funding all but cut off and professions such as medicine and teaching of low status and pay, you're likely to find fairly high-qualified academics, doctors and talented artists doing less-than-fulfilling work, especially in the big cities. A former engineering professor, for example, may be driving a taxi and selling imported kitchenware on the side. When McDonald's opened its first restaurant here, on Pushkin Square in 1990, it received 27,000 applications for 600 hamburger-flipper positions. Hundreds of the applications were from scientists and medical doctors.

Handling Russian Employees

Virtually every Russian who worked for a Soviet-owned enterprise was forced to be deceitful — covering up coworkers' absences and thefts.

Today, Russian employees of foreign companies (especially lower-level clerical and blue collar workers) sometimes feel justified in "ripping off" their employers as a way of "beating the system."

Russians respect power and authority; it's important for foreign businesspeople to firmly establish their own ground rules for honesty and productivity. Don't be conned into doing things "the Russian way." Here are some tips:

- **Adopt a clear mission statement.** Once given a specific task or goal, many Russians will tackle it with bulldog determination. It's up to the employer to show the Russian employee how his role or task is connected to "the big picture" and the future success of the company.

- **Involve employees in decision making.** Be willing to delegate some authority. That way, employees will feel that they have a stake in the success of the company — something they've never had before.

- **Reward initiative.** If employees can see a tangible reward for taking the initiative and are praised among colleagues for doing so, employers can wear down the fear of being innovative and outspoken in the workplace.

- **Provide continual training.** Regardless of a Russian employee's experience, provide ongoing training. It will improve productivity and help attract (and keep) the best and the brightest available.

7 Women in Business

A dog is wiser than a woman. A dog never barks at its master.

— ancient Russian proverb

Second Class Citizens

Although the notion of gender equality, as guaranteed in the old Soviet constitution, was truly revolutionary, it never really manifested in daily life. Women weren't just allowed to work, they were required to, as "social parasites" faced imprisonment. And though Russian women were given the right to vote in 1917 (three years before the 19th Amendment to the U.S. Constitution guaranteed universal suffrage in America), the value of the vote under Soviet rule was dubious.

Russia has always been, and still remains, a male-dominated society, especially in the business world. Though well represented in certain professions (there are more female than male doctors), women remain subservient. At home, women are expected to do it all — often working 40 hours a week in a factory or office, as well as spending an average of 40 hours on such domestic chores as shopping, cooking, housecleaning and laundry, not to mention the time spent caring for her children. By comparison, fathers spent five hours a week on such chores. Since the advent of Capitalism, the plight of the Russian woman has, in many cases, grown worse. For example: Under Soviet law, women were guaranteed 30 percent of the seats in local republic parliaments and city councils (though only one woman ever sat on the Politburo). Today, female representation on local city councils is less than 10 percent.

More than 70 percent of those officially registered as unemployed are women, and according to the Women's Union of Russia (an umbrella group of some 110 women's organizations), almost half of them have university or technical institute degrees. Gone are the government-subsidized prices and childcare that once helped women (especially single mothers) cope. In the new Russia, traditional career paths for women — access to the aforementioned degrees and to government-guaranteed employment — no longer exist. Today, even entry-level jobs for women have strings attached.

The Secretary as Concubine

In Russia, women within the business environment are most frequently seen as lures for capturing new clients or as concubines for management. Classified advertisements for secretaries openly seek women with such vital business attributes as "long legs," "under age 25," or "elegant appearance" and are filled with code phrases such as "prepared to do other duties related to client entertainment." But this should come as no surprise in a country that once held televised vacuum cleaner races to celebrate International Women's Day — a day meant to honor the contribution of women to world culture.

"Women over 40 have been thrown out of the workforce," observes one counselor at Moscow's Gender Center. "These new businessmen don't care about job performance. They're looking for ornaments."

The rule of thumb is fairly simple: if a management job opens up, it's reserved for a man. First, because a man is by tradition the family breadwinner and second because a woman's true place is believed to be in the home. As a general rule, when the employment situation becomes tight, female employees are let go, regardless of their qualifications or performance records.

Historical Conspiracy

It was war, rather than any philosophy of gender equality, that brought Russian women into the workplace to begin with. In the early 1920s, women made up about 25 percent of the labor force, but by 1945, following devastating losses by the Red Army in World War II, Russian women comprised 56 percent. However, the constitutionally mandated "equal pay for equal work" was a myth. The vast majority of women simply couldn't *find* "equal work." They were concentrated in three low-status, low-paying professions — teaching, medicine, and the light manufacturing sector (the latter a low priority in a system that virtually ignored consumer goods).

In the new Russia, male chauvinism continues to shut women out of any meaningful roles in business. While several female entrepreneurs have cracked the male business fraternity, they're very much the exception to the rule. Most women with lower- to middle-level management positions work for foreign-owned companies.

Strategies For Foreign Businesswomen

Although Russian women in the business world aren't taken seriously, the same isn't true for foreign businesswomen. Russian males prefer doing business with other men, but they're worldly enough to appreciate that not all cultures concur.

Don't make the mistake of interpreting what Russian males view as common European courtesies — opening doors for women, complimenting their appearance, even paying their tab — as condescension. Like pubescent school boys, Russian males (especially those over the age of 40) will be on their best behavior when a lady is present. Those under the age of 35 are much more comfortable with the prospect of gender equality in the workplace than their older counterparts.

A little harmless flirtation (if there is such a thing) can go a long way. Trying to be asexual will not get you very far very fast, nor will it earn you respect or help your business prospects.

One word of warning: Russians (both young and old) make lousy drunks. After a night of welcoming toasts, the level of sexual innuendo is likely to increase. Take any ensuing remarks in stride. If someone oversteps the mark, offer a stern but brief rebuff, but avoid a lecture on political correctness or U.S.-style feminism (it could be a deal killer). If worse comes to worse, make a polite excuse about being overly tired and leave the party. You won't be penalized the next day.

8 Making Connections

Relationships First

Business can be anything but impersonal in Russia. Russians are reluctant to deal with anyone they haven't met face-to-face, regardless of how many telephone calls you may have made or faxes and e-mails you've sent. The relatively slow pace of meetings, the mountains of small talk and the post-meeting "booze-a-thons," while seeming unproductive on the surface, are all part of relationship building. Without a strong personal relationship, it's unlikely that a deal will stand the test of time or survive a better offer from another foreigner partner.

Russian businesspeople view contracts as declarations of intent that may change as the situation changes, rather than as binding agreements. Since Russian business law contains few contract enforcement mechanisms, most business is conducted on the strength of personal relationships. Your best defense — and strongest suit — is a solid personal friendship with your Russian counterpart.

A Local Partner Is Essential

It's virtually impossible to do business without a local Russian partner. Choose wisely; the wrong partner can doom an enterprise before it starts. Even if you have no plans to immediately manufacture or distribute products in Russia, you'll still need a local partner/facilitator to make introductions and set up contacts (and possibly to fend off mafia racketeers and protection scammers down the road). Be aware that a formal partnership agreement may not be needed, since the quality of your informal personal relationship with your primary Russian contact is viewed as being more important than anything put in writing. You'll probably be faced with a choice between two types of Russian partners — the "old," people of more mature stature who earned their stripes under Communism and may have managed a small factory or government ministry department; and the "new," younger entrepreneurs eager to make a few *bucksi* (Russian slang for money), no matter what it takes. Get references and, if possible, do a background check on any potential partner.

Beware of Russians who promise that they can do anything or who claim to have high-level contacts. As the Russian mafia continues to grow, criminal elements are getting more and more involved in businesses, and they're hungry for "legitimate" foreign contacts. Also, beware the Russian partner who boasts of having a large cash reserve and is prepared to finance a deal or a business. The origin of the cash hoard should be thoroughly investigated, for obvious reasons.

Consulting: Big Business

Those with only a rudimentary knowledge of the Russian market shouldn't rely on local Russian consultants alone. Consider hiring both a local consultant and one from your home country who has a track record of successful dealings with Russians (or a quality foreign firm that has a record of being able to deliver the goods). While the locals may "walk the walk and talk the talk," they probably don't have a full grasp of what a Western business person's needs are.

Written Introductions

Russians love official-looking paper. It gives a business deal an air of legitimacy in their minds. All correspondence should be in both your native tongue and in Russian. Don't expect any timely action to a written introduction that hasn't been accompanied by a face-to-face contact. In any written introduction, try and give as much detail about your company and its key players as possible. Russians are impressed by brand names and firms that have dealings with global powerhouses. They're also impressed by education. Mention any higher degrees that company officers have earned, especially if they're from a prestigious business school or university.

9 Strategies for Success

New To The Game

The Russians desperately need outside investment, as well as help in adapting to a market economy, but keep in mind that they have an enormous amount of national pride and less than a decade's worth of business experience. Tread lightly and show respect. A know-it-all attitude with stern lectures about doing things "the American way" or the "German way" will breed animosity and kill the cooperative spirit.

Russia has already moved beyond the infant start-up stage of Capitalism. The economy has matured and Russian businesspeople realize that it takes more than just a good idea and a little venture capital to succeed. Many are realizing that Western-style management practices and organizations are now necessary if they're to build on their initial successes. If presented with the proper sensibilities (minus a patronizing attitude), Russians will lap up the knowledge — though putting it into practice will still require breaking down some cultural barriers.

Ten Golden Rules

- **Build relationships.** Cold calls won't work. Doing business here requires entertaining and getting involved in the personal lives of your counterparts. Without the right local partner, you may be heading for a disaster; attempting to master the tangled web of the new Capitalism on your own is a mistake.

- **Do your homework.** Though they may be pessimistic by nature, Russians will likely prove overly optimistic in their assessment of the market or the prospects for a deal. Often, they'll promise more than they can deliver. Do your homework; be wary if a deal sounds too good or a partner promotes his or her self as flawless. Nothing in Russia goes as smoothly as promised.

- **Avoid dangerous involvements.** The Russian mafia dominates many businesses. It's best to avoid getting involved with such controversial and highly competitive commodities as alcohol and cigarettes. In most retail-level businesses, it's almost impossible to avoid some contact with organized crime, either as protector or supplier. Safer businesses include advertising, law and consulting.

- **Start simply.** Russians prepare for meetings and you should too. However, being prepared doesn't mean that you should overwhelm Russians with facts and figures, at least initially. Keep it simple. Explain concepts and broad goals. Russians put little stock in hard figures (a hangover from the Soviet days, when national economic statistics were meaningless). The time will come to talk nuts and bolts at a later date.

- **Be patient but persistent.** The Russians were brought up in a command economy, wherein the government or the top boss made major decisions. Individual initiative was rarely rewarded — and in most cases, punished. Don't expect miracles or even minor decisions to happen overnight.

McDonald's Corporation spent 12 years in negotiation before opening its first restaurant here, on Pushkin Square. Though several more have since opened in Moscow, the Pushkin Square restaurant remains one of the most profitable McDonald's in the world; on any Saturday night, its waiting lines are longer than those in front of Lenin's Red Square tomb. (Also central to McDonald's success is its policy of hiring locals — rather than expatriates — to fill decision-making positions, of developing local suppliers, and of adapting their products to suit local tastes.)

Russians will take advantage of a foreigner who seems too eager to conclude an agreement. It may take months and mountains of follow-up letters and faxes to overcome the inertia, but persistence does pay off.

• **Just say "no."** Russians will probably pester you to sign some sort of informal protocol or agreement at the very start of your relationship. Just say no. Though your potential Russian partner may insist that such a protocol carries no legal weight (he's probably right, considering the state of business law in the country), avoid such agreements like the plague — they may bind you under law to sign a more detailed agreement later. Instead, try to work informally with your partner for several months to make sure the relationship works.

• **Build a strong team of local managers.** A real deal sweetener (and an insurance policy of sorts) is for the foreign partner to include comprehensive management training for locals. The largest business success stories in the country — McDonalds and Britain's Allied Domecq PLC (which includes Baskin-Robbins ice cream, Dunkin' Donuts, and John Bull pubs) — owe much of their good fortune to a strong management trainee program. These programs go beyond just schooling to include newly minted managers in decision-making and planning.

- **Maintain solid business ethics.** Bribery and payoffs may provide initial shortcuts through the maze, but once word gets out that you're willing to travel this route, the cost of business will escalate. Your initial shortcut may evolve into a long-term nightmare.

   Be aware that many Russians believe that their country is used as a dumping ground for shoddy and/or obsolete Western goods. Avoid any business dealings that might encourage this belief.

- **Know your legal options.** Before beginning talks have some idea of which corporate structure will work best for your business (the tax advantages or penalties can be enormous), and seek out partners who suit that structure. Regulatory business law in Russia is rather poorly developed at present, and legalities can literally change on a daily basis. Seek out a good attorney with local experience and a solid reputation.

- **Keep your sense of humor — and get everything in writing**. Cultural shock is inevitable (even for frequent travelers), so it's important to maintain a sense of humor. Don't sweat the small things and try to have fun. Paranoia can ruin a good business deal. Also, because of the inherent dangers of relying on translators (especially with a language as imprecise as Russian), it's important to follow up presentations or meetings with written correspondence (in both Russian and your native language) to prevent misunderstandings.

A Note on Gift-Giving

Russians are very fond of gifts. A small, thoughtful gift for business associates or their families will not only be greatly appreciated, it will be more or less expected. Ideally, it should be personalized somehow; a pen or a cigarette lighter with your company's logo on it would be considered by many to be the perfect gesture, or perhaps a solar-powered calculator. You can be sure it will be well used, if only to allow your Russian business partner to brag to fellow Russians about his foreign connections every time he uses it in public. And expect to receive something in return. Even in these highly commercialized times, it's more the thought than the value of the gift that counts.

10 Time

Deadlines: A Foreign Concept

Russians don't equate time with money, though "New Russian" businessmen seem to have a slightly better appreciation of its value than their older countrymen. Meetings are almost always late (under the Soviet system, no one could be fired for tardiness) and often run much longer than originally planned. Patience, rather than punctuality, is the virtue here.

Part of the Russian attitude toward time stems from the country's agrarian background — historically, time was measured in terms of seasons (planting, growing and harvesting) rather than in days, hours or minutes. Also, the vastness of Russia spans 11 time zones (but all trains run on Moscow time), and the relative backwardness of its internal communications network meant that meeting deadlines was a less critical element in commerce than it was in the West. (Keep in mind that only a few years ago, a citizen would have to wait more than five years for the delivery of a new car after it was purchased and ten to twelve years to obtain a private telephone line.)

"Every business meeting in Russia seems to take forever," laments one Moscow-based American executive. "They really are social occasions. No one seems to care much if an hour's meeting turns into a two-hour affair. I always wonder about the poor guy waiting for his turn in the next office. I can't tell you on how many occasions that has been *me* — sitting there cooling my heels while the meeting before mine goes into triple overtime. If I want to see two customers in the same day, I schedule one meeting in the early morning and one in the late afternoon. It's the only way of having any chance of making the connection."

Because of this casual approach, Russians aren't particularly appreciative of having strict time deadlines stipulated in business contracts. So when framing them, expect delays and leave yourself plenty of "wiggle" room.

Social Functions

Theater performances, cinema screenings and sports events do start on time, but it's rare indeed when a Russian is on time for a social occasion, especially at a public venue like a restaurant. And once they do arrive, don't expect them to leave early. Dinner can often drag on into the wee hours of the morning.

Being late isn't considered rude or boorish behavior. However, if you're invited to a Russian's home for dinner, do try and get there within a half hour of the requested arrival time.

Business Meetings

The Fax Of Life

Trying to arrange a business meeting in Russia can rapidly age even the most patient of entrepreneurs. Telecommunications, even in the largest Russian cities, can be somewhat spotty, and as you'll learn, Russian secretaries simply don't take phone messages. (They say they will, but they almost never write anything down. One good defense: Ask them to read the message back to you. However, if there's not a common language, there's no point in telephoning.)

While the telephone and e-mail are acceptable modes of communication here, faxes are probably the best and most reliable method. And they allow you to use company letterheads — an important point for Russians, who value paperwork and official looking documents. All faxes should be sent in both your native language and in Russian. Don't simply rely on a telephone confirmation of a meeting — get it in writing. Patience is essential; even with a fixer or Russian agent on the ground, actually getting a fixed time when all the officials of a particular company you wish to see will be available will take some doing. Don't expect to throw together a trip in a matter of days or even weeks.

One word of warning: Meetings often get canceled with little notice, and on occasion the wrong people have been known to show up. Losing your temper won't help, but a modest show of indignation and refusing to take *Nyet* for an answer will lead to a rescheduling, hopefully one that suits you.

Be Prepared

Don't underestimate Russian knowledge or their business instinct. A poorly conceived or poorly explained proposal (one that hasn't been properly researched in the Russian marketplace) can ruin your credibility, even before the first round of drinks. Also, a rudimentary knowledge of the country's history and geography is essential, as these topics are certain to come up in conversation sooner or later.

It's best to agree on an agenda beforehand. And in order to frame the discussion and maintain some control, it's wise to be the first to propose a draft (in writing). By all means ask your Russian counterparts for their input.

Let the Russians know the names and titles of those who'll be attending the meeting. Russians don't like surprises. Make a point of sending an official who is at the same level as the most senior Russians you expect to meet. And don't send too many people, as this will overwhelm your hosts.

It used to be that first meetings had a precise sequence — such as an introductory session, a tour of the facilities or offices if appropriate, an official lunch and a wrap-up discussion. Today, this happens much less often, as the comings and goings of foreign business visitors are everyday occurrences.

The Arrival

Only the very brave rent a self-drive vehicle in major cities. Consider hiring a local driver with his or her own car. Don't rely on taxis or public transportation. If the company you're meeting with is large or prosperous enough, they'll probably send a driver to your hotel. Russians have a casual approach to time, but they hold foreigners to a higher standard and will expect you to be on time, even if they can't see you immediately.

The security at many offices resembles that of banks — or prisons. You may be asked to pass through a metal detector or if you would mind being frisked. Some meetings take place behind bullet-proof glass. To deter crime and harassment from protection rackets, many Moscow businesses have moved to small, nondescript buildings.

While your hosts will be eager to shake your hand, it's considered bad luck to extend your hand before crossing the threshold of a room. Also, if for some reason you're met in the building lobby, don't attempt to shake hands with your gloves on. It's considered an insult.

The Business Card Ritual

Russians put great stock in the exchange of business cards. One reason for this is that comprehensive, up-to-date telephone directories (especially in the burgeoning major cities) aren't always available. Your cards should be in both your native language and in Russian, and it's essential that they include your title. Study any card you've been handed before putting it away, and always have plenty of cards yourself. Everyone present at the meeting will expect to receive one.

Meeting Protocol

It should be clear with the introductions (and the advance exchange of faxes and letters) just who's in charge. That person will be seated at the head of the table and will generally have a few underlings (looking too eager to serve) standing by.

While your hosts may ramble on somewhat and wander from the meeting's set agenda, it's offensive to interrupt a presentation. Wait until after the speaker has finished before raising any questions or objections. Your own presentation should be crisp and not too overburdened with statistics. Speak of overall visions and generalities, avoid unnecessary jargon (it won't be understood), and be prepared to address questions specific to the Russian marketplace.

If you can't tolerate cigarette smoke, you're in trouble. Though imported brands are popular, many still smoke such local stinkos as *Cosmos* and *Sputnik*. Russians considered it extremely rude and offensive to ask anyone to stop smoking. Your only hope would be to have a woman in your party. Russian males will usually refrain if a woman politely makes it known that she's allergic to the smoke.

Concessions Over Dessert

Leave it to your hosts to decide when a meeting has concluded. Even if the atmosphere has been rather formal and stuffy, it's possible to leave in a flurry of warm, bone-crushing handgrips and backslaps that could knock out your dentures — signs that your presentation was well received. If you're invited to a private home or restaurant on a spur of the moment, by all means accept. To refuse is to insult, and besides, social occasions allow for the personal relationship building that business here depends on. And it's possible that the Russian who "stonewalled" you during the meeting will happily concede any number of points over dessert.

Interpreters: The Key
To Success Or Failure

The study of foreign languages in Russia was once the domain of the privileged Communist elite. Today, most of those who speak English (or any other foreign language) well enough to act as an interpreter probably learned and developed their skills courtesy of the Communist Party, with the aim of keeping an eye on visiting foreigners. Some of the best are former military intelligence officers. Many consider themselves to be underemployed and/or smarter than the two principles for whom they're negotiating.

You'll be expected to supply your own interpreter; ask a trusted colleague for references. Make clear what your interpreter's role is and that you need to know *everything* that's said. Editing by an interpreter can make or break negotiations. It's essential to hire someone who has the technical expertise to translate in your field. (Be aware that many Russian words used in commerce, even such Western adaptations as *kontract*, have different shades of meaning to different Russians.) There are Russian agencies that specialize in supplying interpreters in such highly technical areas as oil and gas exploration, computer hardware and software, and machine building. The value of a good and trusted interpreter can't be overemphasized.

12   Negotiating with Russians

When it comes to business dealings, there is a perception that Russians are very secretive and not to be trusted. The lack of a business tradition and any semblance of an enforceable business law contributes to this perception. Russians do tend to play their cards close to the chest and business loyalty is for sale to the highest bidder.

Chess Anyone?

Russians are quick to size up the strengths and weaknesses of adversaries and to take ruthless advantage of any opportunities that present themselves. Time is always on their side, and they believe they'll eventually get the best of anyone who's in a hurry.

Probably the single-most-important thing to remember about the Russians is that they are zero-sum thinkers — that is, *they believe that they can win only if the other side loses*. Trying to convince them of the merits of a "win-win" strategy is a waste of time and energy, and compromise is seen as weakness. Their habit of circumventing established rules and seeking out loopholes are remnants of the

Communist system (and before that, of feudalism). Keep in mind that Russians are among the greatest chess players in the world; they have a talent for thinking several moves in advance.

"We had been talking with a scientific research company for months and the negotiations seemed to be on course, when suddenly the Russians just stopped talking to us and we couldn't figure out why," recalls a Moscow-based American business-man. "We spent months pursuing them to resume the talks and just as suddenly as they'd stopped, they started again, right where they left off. It took us a while to figure out what they were playing at. Then we realized the idea was to try and wear us out. They were purposely avoiding contact, count-ing on our frustration and exhaustion from pursu-ing them to give them an advantage and wring more concessions from us."

"We learned," he continued, "that while you may not understand their behavior or think it's rational, it's all part of a long-term strategy to win. What may look like a crazy turn of events is really part of the chess game."

To succeed, you need to be thick-skinned, determined, patient, and armed with a sense of humor. And it's essential that your team present a united front.

Expect The Unexpected

One thing you can probably count on is being asked to present your side first. Russians prefer to know the other person's position in full before revealing their own. From the opening gambit on, remember: Expect the unexpected — including having the Russians make dire proclamations that the deal's off as they walk out of the room. Other negotiation ploys you may encounter include:

• **The off-the-wall opening gambit.** Often, Russians will assume what amounts to a ludicrous initial position. One French businessman recalls the Russian side proposing a deal that would have had the French company assume virtually all of the risk and provide all of the start-up capital, only to earn about 10 percent of potential profits. "It took everything within my power to convince Paris that this was just an opening ploy and that the Russians weren't serious. It took months and scores of revisions but we eventually got what we considered to be a fair deal, one that bore no resemblance to what the Russians had initially proposed."

Don't be tempted to give in or simply to demand minor changes. If you do, you can expect even more outrageous demands down the road; the Russians will assume that you don't have the stomach for tough talks or that you value the deal's completion too highly to seek the best terms. Consider throwing out your own wildly outrageous starting point and talk down from there.

• **You (or people like you) have cheated us.** Russians will tell you that your company or a similar one has cheated them in the past, missed deadlines, and misled them on contract terms. They may go so far as to condemn foreign businesspeople in general as conniving and less than fair. The idea here is to stir up feelings of guilt or remorse and to get you to soften your position. Don't fall for it. Counter with your own laundry list of broken Russian promises and deceit (all with a relatively matter of fact tone). But avoid personal recriminations; they'll kill the deal. If worse comes to worse, apologize for past (alleged) behavior and say you're ready to move on with a fresh start.

- **Business as social work.** Be prepared to hear tales of woe — about everything from sickly babies to hundreds (if not thousands) of workers potentially losing their jobs if the deal fails. You may be an entire village's last hope! Your adversary is trying to transform your business agenda into social work and philanthropy. Listen sympathetically, but don't allow your heart strings to be tugged too severely. The simple response — that a good deal will help to "float everyone's boat," poor villagers included — is an effective counter.

- **Stall ball.** Russians have patience and they'll use your eagerness against you, by delaying talks in the hope of extracting further concessions. You may spend months negotiating with someone you thought had decision-making power, only to be told, "I don't have the authority." Take a deep breath and recognize this for what it is — a stall tactic aimed at breaking down your resistance.

- **Secrecy.** Even before the Soviet era, Russians had a great penchant for secrecy; the Communist-era information blackout only reinforced it. Russians won't reveal everything about their company, finances, staff, competitors or other suitors, so don't feel obliged to tell *them* everything. Do as much homework on a company as you can (it may be difficult, because of the lack of proper disclosure laws), but don't expect to get an honest assessment of the company or the industry from the Russians you're negotiating with — even if such a disclosure might be in their favor.

The End Game

Russians have a good sense of just how far they can push an adversary without killing a deal. Don't be afraid to call their bluff. Announcing that you're not prepared to make any more concessions and that no agreement is better than a poor one can produce a surprising amount of flexibility, especially if the Russians sense that you're serious. Even in the absence of a detailed transaction, the Russians may want you to sign an "agreement in principle," a summation and interpretation of what was discussed. Proceed with caution. Regardless of how harmless this sounds, it may obligate you to a more structured deal down the road or tie your hands when seeking other in-country deals.

Always look for problems in written documents. Translation can be imprecise and the whole sense or structure of a deal can be altered by the use or substitution of a single word. (And be aware that intellectual property rights agreements are a new concept here.) Documents and contracts are usually provided in both Russian and your own native tongue; both versions are considered valid. However, it's essential that you have a fluent Russian speaker compare the translations to ensure that there's no ambiguity.

Still, even if you have a signed contract, it may not be worth much. As previously noted, Russians see contracts more as statements of intent than formally binding obligations with penalties. Though it's improving, Russian business law still isn't sophisticated enough (or stable enough) to deal with suits stemming from broken contracts. In the case of joint ventures, consider including a clause requiring all partners to submit to arbitration in a neutral third country (such as Sweden) in case of disagreement.

Business Outside the Law

The Mafia

Many Russians claim that the Russian mafia virtually runs the country. Criminal gangs are involved in everything from running protection rackets, prostitution rings and sports clubs to controlling commodity trading and stealing weapons-grade uranium. They're also running "legitimate" enterprises; the Interior Ministry claims that gangs (the mafia consists of several competing organizations) control at least 40,000 businesses in Russia, including 500 banks. Russian authorities estimate that of the US$43 billion that the country invested abroad in 1995, at least $18 billion of it had been earned by the Russian mafia.

According to *Forbes Magazine*, "assassination is a tool of business competition" here; contract killings are another mafia specialty. In 1995, for example, some 40,000 Russians were murdered and another 70,000 disappeared. Among the former were banker Ivan Kivelidi, founder of the Russian Business Roundtable (an obscure nerve toxin had been applied to the rim of his coffee cup) and Vladislav Listiev, the country's most popular talk show host and most successful TV producer. Two weeks after Listiev announced his intention to clean up corruption within his industry, he was gunned down, by professionals, at the entrance to his apartment. Despite public outrage, such crimes are unlikely to be resolved.

No longer content to reap profits from the chaotic transition from Communism to Capitalism, the mafia has gone international. The U.S. Congress has held hearings on the workings of the Russian mob in the U.S., and several European nations (Britain and France included) have been cooperating with Russia's government to stem the influence of Russian crooks in their own countries.

These gangs didn't spring up following the demise of Communism like daisies in the desert after a rainfall. They were always there to some extent, running the "black" (illegal) and "gray" (unethical but not illegal) markets. With the breakdown of law and order, they simply took advantage of their experience in the unsavory, reaping the financial rewards of a nascent, free market economy.

The Krysha

Krysha (literally, roof) is what Russians call "protectors" who shelter businesses from criminal elements. Sometimes, the *krysha* is the criminal gang itself, other times it's a legitimate security firm. If necessary, one *krysha* will strike a deal with another *krysha*. Some seek out official rulings to end disputes; others resort to violence. A "roof" can mean the difference between success and bankruptcy, especially for a business that handles a lot of cash. According to the Russian Chamber of Commerce, upward of 70 percent of all local businesses say they pay money to organized crime — 10 to 25 percent of their profits, on average.

"Within days of opening up, we'd had 'offers' of protection from three or four different hoodlum gangs," recalls a foreign manager of a Moscow restaurant. "We checked around and picked the most feared of the hoods as our *krysha*. It takes a whack out of profits, right off the top, but we haven't been bothered by anyone since. It's a legitimate business expense."

About 20 to 30 percent of foreign corporations in Russia (usually those dealing on a retail level) have faced extortion demands. For the most part, foreigners remain off the target list of professional Russian hitmen. However, threats of kidnapping and physical violence have caused at least some companies to rethink the number of Russia-based foreigners they wish to employ.

The Rising Price of Payoffs

Gone are the days when you could bribe your way through Customs or make friends in government circles with the gift of a pocket calculator or radio. Today, the asking price is cash (usually equivalent to thousands of U.S. dollars) for such things as permits and customs clearances. Many Communist Party officials have evolved into businessmen and, in the spirit of the new Russia, they demand kickbacks for contracts — using the pocket calculators they acquired in the old days to add up their new fortunes. Police have the right to stop anyone on the street for a random document check, and there's evidence that such checks include emptying out the wallets of foreign visitors. Traffic police (the GAI) also have a racket going — arresting foreigners for jaywalking and then demanding a fine of US$100 in lieu of a night in jail. During the good old days of the Soviet regime, a mere US$5 would diffuse an encounter with the GAI.

Street Crime: Gypsies & Thieves

Russia has the world's highest rate of imprisonment, with 558 inmates per 100,000 population. (The U.S. ranks second with 519 per 100,000, while Indonesia is last with just 22 inmates per 100,000.) Still, between 1995 and 1997, the number of crimes against foreigners in Moscow dropped 14 percent, and in St. Petersburg, overall street crime dropped 18 percent. St. Petersburg has launched a special tourist police force. Known as the *gorodoviye*, these English-speaking officers who wear red hats have been instrumental in curbing crime against visitors.

A few safety tips:

- Beware of so-called gypsies, homeless people and/or professional con artists who approach pedestrians, begging. On occasion, dozens of little waifs will swarm the unwary. Don't be afraid to scream, yell and swear, but resist striking out. Their aim is to get your hand off your wallet and they're very good at it.

- Use only official taxis and never get into a taxi that already has a passenger inside. This is a common mugging scam.

- Never ride in empty subway cars at night, and stick to the cars in the middle of the train.

Moonshine & Drugs

In one nine-month period between 1996 and 1997, Russian police confiscated 80,000 tons of illegal alcohol. They estimate that about 40 percent of all the vodka sold here is produced from illegally imported spirits, and not all of it up to quality standards. It's no surprise that the number of alcohol poisoning deaths has climbed 227 percent in recent years. (If unsure of the origin of your alcohol, abstain. It could give you more than a hangover.)

Illegal drugs, virtually unheard of in the Communist era, have become a serious threat to law and order (though the number of addicts is still small compared to many Western countries). With Russia's once tightly sealed borders now relatively porous, marijuana and opium make their way into the large cities quite easily; the ancient Silk Road, which traverses several ex-Soviet republics, has become one of the world's primary "heroin highways," a key transit route for drugs headed West from Asia. Also, the Russian Mafia does a good job in laundering cash; Interpol has traced Russian involvement in drug cartels as far afield as Japan and South America.

Sex and the Single (or Married) Russian

The Russians have belatedly discovered the sexual revolution and sex has become a national obsession, second only to alcohol. Though technically illegal, prostitution is rampant. Russian hookers run the gamut from weary streetwalkers to high-class call girls who charge three to four hundred U.S. dollars a night. Many will lower their rates for men they're physically attracted to, or they may refuse to accommodate a nonwhite male or insist on charging him double or triple the going rate.

14   Names & Greetings

Russians are still somewhat unsure about how they should address each other in a post-Communist world. The one-size-fits-all greeting of *tovarich* (comrade) has given way to foreign imports and pre-revolutionary greetings (such as "ladies and gentlemen") that have been in linguistic mothballs for decades.

Formality Rules

Russians may appear warm, friendly and physical (rather rigorous handshakes, backslaps, bear hugs or kisses) in their greetings, but don't underestimate their need for formality when it comes to dealing with foreign businesspeople. Often in initial encounters, Russians will address you using your business title, such as "Company Director Smith" or "Company Treasurer Jones." You should do likewise. Though it may sound awkward, the use of titles (Director-General Koslov) is the accepted norm. If in doubt, refer to the business card you've been given.

Generally speaking, addressing a Russian solely by his or her first name is an insult. (However, this is becoming more popular among younger Russians, especially those dealing with Americans.) When addressing foreigners, Russians often use such courtesy titles as *Gospodin* (Mr.) and *Gospozha* (Mrs.). If you're speaking Russian, be sure to use the more formal *vy* form, rather than the informal *ty*.

Honor Thy Father

Russian names are listed in same order as in the West: first name (*imya*), middle name (*otchestvo*) and last name (*familiya*). The quirk is that the Russian middle name is a patronymic — a name derived from the first name of one's father. Take the name Mikhail Sergievich Gorbachev. Sergievich literally means "son of Sergie."

Russian women add the letter "a" to the end of their family name, to their husband's last name (which they adopt upon marriage), and to their patronymic. For example: Raisa Gorbachev (Mikhail's wife) is known in Russian as Raisa Maximovna Gorbacheva, her patronymic meaning "daughter of Maxim." The Western media often drop the feminine "a", a practice that Russians find very annoying.

Beyond the Formal Stage

Once Russians move beyond the initial formal stage of a relationship, they use the first name and patronymic only. This doesn't necessarily signify a close friendship, but it's a clear indication that the relationship is moving ahead.

Your Russian counterpart will eventually invite you to address him or her by their patronymic. To not do so after having been invited to is an insult. This is the time to suggest that your Russian host address you by your first name. Once this barrier is broken, use the patronymic for all communications, including written ones.

Big Kolya: Diminutives & Nicknames

Among friends, Russians use nicknames and a rather confusing array of diminutives (cute little forms of first names) that often bare no resemblance whatsoever to the name from which they were derived. For example: Shasha and Shura are diminutive forms of Alexander; Vanya is the diminutive of Ivan; and Kolya is short for Nickolai. For women, there seems to be a little more logic, with Luda short for Ludmilya and Tanya for Tatiana. Compared to many cultures, there isn't a wide variation of first names available; pedigrees like Ivan Ivanovich Ivanov aren't uncommon. In the workplace, you'll often have several people with the same first name and the same patronymic. As surnames are almost never used in informal situations, Russians rely on nicknames. If, for example, there are two Nickolai Nickoliavichs, the older of the two will be call Big Kolya and the younger one, Young Kolya.

On an historical note: In Communism's heyday, many Russians gave children such inspirational names as Tractor, Melor (an acronym for Marx, Engles, Lenin, October Revolution) or even Ninel (a girl's name that's actually Lenin spelled backwards). This practice was more popular in the countryside and has, of course, ceased since the demise of Communism. Many of these unfortunately named offspring have since adopted more common first names.

15 Communication Styles

Privacy?

Communication here is a contact sport. There's no word for privacy in the Russian language, and the Russians you encounter will have no regard for personal space. In conversation, they'll edge ever closer until they're literally in your face. On the subway or in crowded public venues, Russians wedge their way through throngs with nary a word of apology.

Don't Take Neyt For An Answer

Ask a question and you'll invariably receive *nyet* (no) for an answer. Sometimes it will be gruff, other times more civil. This is because, historically, innovation was discouraged and no one wanted to be held responsible for a project or request that might fail. This habitual response is also a hangover from the era of shortages and backroom deals on the retail level, when store clerks always seemed to have extra stock hidden away. The first response to a question about something's availability would always be *nyet*, a signal for the negotiations to begin.

Russians routinely refuse to accept *neyt* for an answer, and so should you. It may simply mean that the person who's replying needs some incentive to produce the goods or time to think through your proposition.

"You learn this lesson fairly quickly," explains a British consultant based in St. Petersburg. "It happens for theater tickets, airline tickets, train tickets, at restaurants, virtually everywhere. Their first response is 'No, that's impossible. We don't have what you want.' Usually within ten minutes, I've negotiated two of the best seats in the house, with the help of a little under-the-table 'commission'. It's the only way."

Long Winded

Even the simplest question is likely to elicit a long-winded answer that may leave you baffled or actually knowing less than when you asked the question. Be patient. Russians like to be very thorough when answering queries.

If caught in a debate or argument, you can avoid an escalation by letting Russian long-windedness act in your favor. Don't interrupt the diatribe; let them exhaust themselves in emotion, historical explanation and rationale. Once they've spoken their piece, you'll find that they're likely to feel a lot less strongly than they did when the disagreement started, and they may even be willing to compromise (or at least see some value in your position).

Normalno

When there's a crisis, Russians aren't likely to acknowledge it — at least not to foreigners. This is an aspect of Russian stoicism. The expression *normalno* — everything is normal or status quo — is a favorite one used to deny the extraordinary. Russians will reply *normalno* if you ask how they're feeling, even if they've just come out of triple by-pass heart surgery.

During the 1986 Chernobyl power plant disaster in the Ukraine, senior Soviet officials insisted on referring to the situation as *normalno*, even after having admitted that there had been a nuclear radiation leak. An American journalist based in Moscow recalls that back in the late 1980s, when a young German pilot named Matthius Rust evaded Soviet radar on a flight from Finland and managed to land his small Cessna aircraft just a few yards from the Kremlin, the militia guarding the aircraft refused to admit that anything unusual had occurred.

"The plane was in the middle of Red Square, 200 feet from where we were standing. When I asked the militiaman what was going on, he said, *"Normalno."* So I asked him to turnaround and look at the plane. He stared at it for a few minutes and then replied again, straight faced, "Oh that, it's *normalno.*"

Communication Tips

- **Saving Face**

Although they may appear to be thick-skinned and stoic, Russians are very sensitive when it comes to issues of personal pride. Criticism of a proposal or an idea is a sure way to kill a relationship. Never say things like "That doesn't make sense" or "You're wrong and we have the figures to prove it." Such unconstructive criticism will cause a Russian to "lose face," and like the proverbial elephant, Russians have long memories.

Be constructive; instead of openly criticizing an idea or proposal, make a counterproposal. And leave the Russian with some "wiggle room," so that he or she doesn't have to admit to an error, at least publicly.

- **Profanity**

Whether in business or in social conversations, avoid using foul language. Russians are very conservative when it comes to curse words, especially when a female is present. Great stock is placed in one's deportment and credibility can be lost. No one wants to be labeled a "hooligan" — the type of urban lowlife Russian who uses such language.

- **Hand Signals**

Avoid the "peace sign" (second and third finger extended in a V shape) delivered with the palm facing inward. It's the equivalent of "giving someone the finger" (middle finger extended) in the West. "Thumbs up" indicates approval.

- **Be Positive**

Avoid broaching negative aspects of Soviet and Russian history. The Russians are extremely proud of their heritage but they can be extremely sensitive about eras that they believe are best forgotten.

- **Jokes**

Russians appreciate a good sense of humor but jokes shouldn't be at their country's expense. Only Russians can make fun of Russia. And keep in mind that jokes don't translate well between cultures.

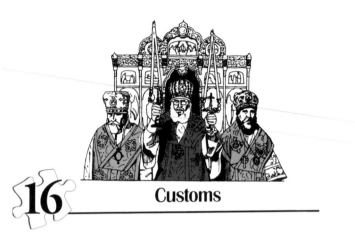

16 Customs

Snovum Godum: Happy New Year

With Revolution Day (which marks the 1917 Bolshevik takeover) and May Day (the international day of labor) being downgraded as national holidays, New Year's Day has emerged as the most important (and joyous) occasion on the Russian calendar.

New Year's Day closely resembles Christmas, with its singing of carols (*kolyadki*), exchanges of gifts, and decorated trees. Grandfather Frost (a dead ringer for Santa), accompanied by a Tinkerbell-like waif known as the Snow Maiden, visits homes to deliver gifts for children. *Kutya* (a mixture of wheatberries, poppy seeds and honey) and *kissel* (a chilled cranberry purée served with cream) are traditional seasonal fare.

Standing Room Only

Russian Orthodox Church services are mystical, tradition-bound and long. Weddings can last three hours and Easter services (complete with the mellifluous chants of a male chorus) five to six hours. Meanwhile, everyone is required to stand;

there are no pews or benches. The gold incense burners and elaborate dress of the bearded priests stand in stark contrast to the relative poverty of the parishioners. Women are expected to cover their heads and to wear skirts of a conservative length.

UFOs & Military Astrologers

Superstition cuts across every strata of society. Widely held beliefs include:

- Bad luck awaits after lighting a cigar from a candle on a restaurant table
- Monday is a bad day to start a journey or a business venture (and Monday morning business meetings are hard to come by)
- A cat should be the first creature to cross the threshold of a new home
- Women (and many believe men, as well) should never sit at the corner of a dinner table; it means that they'll never marry
- Spitting three times over one's shoulder prevents bad news.

"Old wive's tales" are popular, too. Following the 1986 Chernobyl nuclear disaster in Ukraine, word spread that red wine could prevent and cure radiation sickness. So great was the local hysteria that the Soviet government marked the region for additional wine supplies — apparently in lieu of sophisticated medical treatments. There were few complaints, and red wine virtually became a prescription drug.

Russians are advocates of the para-normal. It's believed that, during the Cold War, a Soviet government program was launched to develop a method of mass mind control. (America's C.I.A. took this Russian obsession seriously enough to launch a similar program, an attempt to pre-empt the Russians at their own game.) Today, Russian psychic hotlines are a booming business, as are UFO clubs and societies.

The configuration of planets also holds sway. Both Lenin and Stalin heeded the advice of astrologers, as did Boris Yeltsin. (Brezhnev was a devotee of a faith healer.) According to *The Economist*, a Russian naval captain first class, one Alexander Buzinov, gave a television interview in December of 1997 in which he described his work as a "military astrologer" for a "secret institute." His studies, he claimed, had led him to accurately predict everything from high-end bureaucratic firings to terrorist attacks to the vacillations of Yeltsin's health.

Hair Today, Bald Tomorrow

Many Russians are convinced of the inevitability of a bald man succeeding Boris Yeltsin as the country's leader. Since the end of Czarist rule, the country has been governed, alternatively, by bald reformers and reactionaries with full heads of hair. (True, Yeltsin as a reformer seems to break the pattern, but his efforts to restore law and order may yet be deemed reactionary.)

It began with a bald Lenin leading the 1917 Revolution. He was followed by Stalin (wavy locks), the ultimate paranoid reactionary, who gave way to Nikita Khrushchev, a bald reformer who attempted to undue the worst of Stalin's programs. Khrushchev was dumped by a Politburo that feared reform in favor of Leonid Brezhnev — he of the big hair and bushy eyebrows, who sent Russia careening back to Stalinism. Then Gorbachev (bald as an eagle) came in as the great reformer, followed by the hirsute Yeltsin.

17 Dress & Appearance

The Cachet of Shoes & Watches

Although the country is far from a fashion mecca, Russians have high expectations about the way foreigners, especially businesspeople, should dress. One of the first things they notice are shoes. This dates back to the "bad old days" of the Soviet era, when shoes were *defitsitny* (goods chronically in short supply); those that were available were frumpy and tended to fall apart when wet. Good shoes were imported, and therefore status symbols. Expensive wristwatches have the same cachet.

Conservative is Best

Conservative business suits are appropriate for most occasions, including evenings out. The new Russian elite tend to show off; don't try to match them karat for karat or fur for fur. For women, skirts and dresses are more the norm than pants. Sneakers are only worn at the gym or health club.

High fashion for Russian women tends toward very high heels, tight dresses (often too much Tatiana or Luda stuffed into too little material), heavy makeup and big hair. Wealthy mutton invariably dresses as lamb — a sight that often takes some getting used.

Surviving Winter

When the wind howls and the snow piles up, the only way to survive is by dressing in layers. A good pair of waterproof, insulated boots is essential. It may be well below zero outside, but inside most Russian buildings are unbearable tropical — centrally heated from a common city furnace — there are no individual building boilers or individual thermostats. So few Russians wear sweaters indoors, ever. The heat switches on at a certain date in winter and turns off at a certain date in spring, regardless of actual weather conditions.

The Shapka

These furry round hats are popular with both sexes; no other headwear will keep you as warm outdoors. Just about any type of animal with fur — seals, Persian lambs, dogs, cats, rabbits, even large rodents — has been known to end up as a *shapka*. The hat is almost always worn with the flaps tied up atop the head. Many Muscovites believe that wearing the flaps down is a sign of a particular sexual preference (one that, for men, was punishable by up to five years in the *gulag)*. There's one exception to this unwritten rule: On particularly bone-chilling days (those approaching -30°C or -22°F), a central order goes out from police headquarters authorizing cops on the beat to turn their flaps down over their ears.

Bad Manners

It's *nyekulturny* (uncultured) to wear coats or boots indoors in public buildings — offices, restaurants, theaters and so on — or to hang your coat over the back of your chair. You're expected to check these items in the *garderob* (cloakroom).

18 Reading the Russians

Physical is Good

In business, the general rule of thumb is that should a Russian become demonstratively physical — bear hugs, death-grip handshakes, exuberant backslapping — it means that your meeting went very well and that your personal relationship (the foundation of business deals) is well on its way. A stone face and lack of warm contact are clear indicators that something is amiss.

Traditionally, Russians use body language and hand gestures rather than verbal communication to signify their excitement, approval or disapproval. A famous example is the late Nikita Khrushchev's shoe-banging episode at the United Nations in the 1960s. Russians believe that physical gestures lend drama to simple communications and help to underscore the intensity of feelings.

While many Russian businesspeople will sit pokerfaced during a presentation, their winks and nods can be taken as positive signs.

Few Smiles

European and American businesspeople are apt to be all smiles, beginning a conversation or reaching to shake hands with a smile. For Russians, however, smiles are highly valued and not offered so indiscriminately. (No, it's not true that the chronically poor state of the country's dental health is the real reason behind this severe rationing.)

Try to maintain direct eye contact, even if you're using an interpreter to discuss business. Looking away during a conversation is considered rude and it will cast doubts on your sincerity. If a Russian avoids eye contact, what's being said is probably not to be trusted.

Some Quirks

While Russians shake hands with male counterparts at both the beginning and end of meetings, they will not offer to do so with women. (However, women should feel free to extend their hands when introduced.) If the meeting has gone well, women are likely to get a triple kiss on the cheeks the next time they meet.

While Russians use a lot of hand gestures, they never point or wag a finger across a table.

Entertaining

Vodka

No Russian meal is complete without vodka, which alone accounts for five percent of all retail sales in Russia. (Scotch is gaining favor with successful New Russians.) And yes, it's true that once a bottle has been opened, it must be consumed, but this has more to do with the unavailability of screw tops and re-sealable bottles than with deep-seated tradition. In restaurants, vodka is usually ordered by weight and is served chilled in a small pitcher.

Vodka (literally, little water) was first produced here in the 14th century. Its popularity stems from the fact that it can be distilled from wheat, maize, potatoes, sugar beets or rye — all relatively plentiful in Russia. Tsar Peter the Great was the first to see its potential profit; in the late 18th century, he established the State Monopoly of Vodka, which made the government its sole legal producer.

A word of warning: It's not uncommon, even in upscale restaurants, to witness drunken fist fights and men literally falling over tables onto the laps of total strangers. And the subways are littered with drunks begging for a few *rubles* for another bottle Keep your sense of humor and expect your "space" to be violated. A drunken Russian will swing first and ask questions later.

Caviar Sandwiches

Russia still produces some of the world's finest and most expensive caviar. Despite reports of an impending disaster caused by poaching in and around the Caspian Sea, these smelly little sturgeon fish eggs are still fairly common here, though less so (and less affordable) than 15 or 20 years ago. Russians will dazzle you with stories of how, as little children, they were sent off to school with caviar and black bread sandwiches in their lunch boxes. It was roughly the Soviet equivalent of the American peanut-butter-and-jelly sandwich. Inexpensive caviar was one of the perks of living in Moscow during the Soviet era. During that time, it was easy to spot Moscow's longtime foreign residents at official receptions and functions. They were the ones who ignored the caviar served at such functions and went right for the bed of green leafy lettuce that the caviar was served on. Lettuce was (and still is) a far rarer commodity, especially in wintertime. Caviar remains a staple in restaurants, where it's often served with *blini* (small thin pancakes) and *smyetana* (sour cream).

The Invitation Home

If your relationship is progressing, your Russian counterpart will invite you to his or her home for a meal. This is an offer that can't be refused.

Meals, whether in homes or restaurants, are often grand occasions. Nothing is too good for a guest, even if it means financial hardship for the host. The food seems never-ending (and full of garlic) and the vodka flows like water (which, if it comes from the tap, is more hazardous than the alcohol). Toasts are still the norm, but never propose a toast before the host — it's the height of *nyekulturny.* Business dinners are usually *sans* wives, though this is changing somewhat, especially among the younger generation.

There are a few ground rules to keep in mind:

- Often, you'll be expected to leave your shoes at the door. The host will provide you with a pair of slippers. Use them. Walking around barefoot or stocking feet is *nyekulturny.*

- It's all right to dress casually in a colleague's home, but eschew bluejeans and T-shirts.

- If you're seated before most of the guests arrive, rise when you're finally introduced to them (both male and female) for the first time.

- Never arrive empty-handed. Lavish gifts aren't expected, but flowers for the hostess and a mid-to-expensively priced bottle of wine or a box of chocolates will be appreciated.

- Never point or gesticulate with your knife (or any other implement) while engaged in conversation at table. It's considered the height of rudeness and bad breeding.

- If offered seconds, don't refuse, even if you take only a small helping. It's considered an insult to your host.

Restaurant Dining

Booking a restaurant in the old days used to be half the battle — the other half being with the surly waiters who would literally throw food at you, as if you were a nuisance. These waiters are still around, but the country has succumbed to an explosion of international restaurants, including French, Mexican and Italian. (Many of the best are patronized by Moscow's burgeoning criminal elite.) The biggest problem now is finding one that won't cost you the equivalent of a month's groceries. Avoid the cheapest of the cheap though, as their hygiene standards are notoriously low. Restaurant hours are generally noon to 3 P.M. for lunch and 7 to 11 P.M. for dinner.

A Few Russian Dishes

Russian cuisine can be tasty, if not exactly sophisticated. Among the choices:

Pelmeni. Little fried dumplings stuffed with mystery meat and left to float in an oil and fat mixture.

Borscht. A red beet soup, usually topped with parsley and sour cream.

Zakuski. The Russian equivalent of Italian antipasto, it's an array of appetizers that includes pickled garlic, cucumbers, green peppers, potatoes, onions, herring, and assorted cold meats.

Kasha. Buckwheat groats.

Chicken Tabak. Like its cousin chicken Kiev, this dish is to be found on most restaurant menus. It is simply breaded fried chicken that looks like it's been run over by a T-72 tank.

Kvaas. Made from fermented black bread, this drink is a summertime favorite. It's served from dispensing machines on the street or from pushcarts.

Maroshennoye. Ice cream. Russian will eat it anytime day or night, winter or summer. The local variety is good but it doesn't come close to those that can be found in the U.S. or Europe.

20 Socializing

The Art of Conversation

Russia boasts a population that's relatively well schooled in its classic literature and philosophy. One Moscow-based American businessman recalls how he shared a train compartment for an overnight trip to St. Petersburg with four Russians — two of them autoworkers — and marveled at their debate over the essence of Yevgeny Yevtushenko's poetry. "I can't think of any other place in the world," he said, "where such a deep conversation could take place among people of such low social rank."

Nightlife?

Well, they aren't exactly Paris or London or New York, but Moscow and St. Petersburg do have some popular nightclubs. (One, near the Kremlin, was described in a local newspaper as having "the highest concentration of beautiful women and heavily armed men in the world.") A cash-rich business, they tend to come and go quickly because of mafia threats and interference. Many nightclubs, casinos and bars *cater* to the Russian mafia; it's best to go with someone who's known there. Avoid the lesser-known night-clubs, which are usually overrun with gun-toting tough guys, prostitutes and drunks. There are also dozens of U.S.-style sports bars, blues clubs and English pubs. While decent places to go for a beer, they're as about as Russian as the Union Jack.

Glued to the Tube

Russians have embraced television, especially now that the steady fare of heroic Soviet movies about comrade workers and documentaries on trac-tor making has been eliminated. Today, Russian TV is a melange of Japanese cartoons, German sports, Mexican *telenovelas*, American commercials and locally produced game shows. Some government officials claim that the final episode of a Brazilian soap opera called *Tropikana* was responsible for the relatively low voter turnout during the last national election. Other favorites are dubbed episodes of the U.S. series *Star Trek* and *Dr. Quinn, Medicine Woman*. The two semi-privatized national broadcast stations — Russian Public Television (ORT), sometimes called the First Channel and Russian Television (RTR), or Channel 2 — reach a combined viewership (both within and beyond Russia's borders) of 350 million.

Movies, too, have become a national obsession. Moscow boasts what is arguably the most profitable single-screen cinema in the world, the Kodak Kino Mir.

The Dacha

Access to a *dacha* or country house (often more a shack than a house) is considered an essential of urban living. On weekends, you can see cars toting families and furniture out of the cities for a few days of digging and planting. More prestigious country homes were once the exclusive privilege of Communist Party favorites. But now, the new Russian elite are building mansions, complete with turrets, in the woods outside major cities.

The resort town of Zelyonaya is using a unique marketing ploy to attract tourists. As Stalin often vacationed here, visitors can now stay in the same summer *dacha* he frequented and sleep in his bed.

Performing Arts

The end of Communism has meant a mini-disaster for the arts. Without government subsidies, the once-proud Bolshoi Theater in Moscow and the Kirov Theater in St. Petersburg have either lost their stars or simply can no longer afford quality productions. (Still, the Bolshoi — literally, "big" — is housed in the magnificent opera house where Mussorgsky's *Boris Gudunov* and Tachaikovsky's *Swan Lake* premiered in the 19th century, and it offers operas and symphonies, as well as ballets.) And the Moscow State Circus is a shadow of its formerly famous self. On the positive side, the end of state control has allowed an explosion of smaller dance and theater groups throughout the country. Most advertise by word of mouth.

Sports Fanatics

Football (soccer) has a large and rowdy following, and the Russian national team is usually one of the better European competitors. Ice hockey is another big draw, but the quality of play has been crippled by the defection of the best players to North American and European professional teams.

As for participation, the Russians, are ... well ... a rather sedentary lot. Tennis is an up-and-coming sport, though courts are few and far between. In winter, ice skating and cross-country skiing are the only escapes many Russians have from a near-fatal dose of cabin fever. Golf is exploding (it seems to go with business deals, even here), with Moscow boasting two relatively new courses and more in the planning stages.

Until the collapse of Communism in 1991, the Soviet Union had but one golf course, in Georgia. It was built especially for U.S. President Dwight Eisenhower, who was hoping to travel to the Soviet Union to attend a summit with Khrushchev. The idea was squashed after an American spy plane was shot down over Russia and the pilot captured. The golf course was apparently never used.

Chess remains the king of sports. Matches are covered as sporting events and analyzed with more scrutiny, by more experts, that an American Super Bowl or a British international cricket match.

Mushroom Picking

It happens every autumn, from August through September. Armed with picnic baskets and buckets, Russians families head out to the forests near Moscow to pick wild mushrooms. What also happens is that scores of Russians perish from eating poisonous ones. Still this ritual is as Russian as baseball is American. If invited to go along, by all means do so. Take along a pair of waterproof boots and refrain from snacking unless you're 100-percent sure of what you're eating.

Basic Russian Phrases

English	Russian
Yes	*Da*
No	*Nyet*
Good	*Horosho*
Bad	*Ploho*
Just okay	*Tak sebe*
Good morning	*Do-bray utro*
Good afternoon	*Do-bray den*
Good evening	*Do-bray vecher*
Good night	*Spo-koyn-oynochi*
Please/You're Welcome	*Pozhaluysta*
Thank you	*Spasibo*
Excuse me?	*Izvinite*
Hello	*Zdra-vst -vyte*
Good bye	*Do svi-dan-ya*
So long	*Poka*

24 Books & Internet Addresses

Russia 2010 and What It Means for the World by Daniel Yergin and Thane Gustafson. Random House, New York, 1993. A thought-provoking look at what the future holds for Russia economically and socially.

Comrade Criminal by Stephen Handelman. Yale University Press, 1997. Handleman is the most authoritative source on the Russian mafia.

In Confidence by By Anatoly Dobrynin. Random House, New York, 1995. Forget all those sugar-coated, self-serving histories of the Cold War written by American politicians. Dobrynin, who was Moscow's man in Washington during the reign of six U.S. presidents, gives the Russian view of dealing with power. This may be the best Cold War history yet written.

The Conquest of a Continent: Siberia and the Russians by W. Bruce Lincoln. Random House, New York, 1994. A fascinating adventure story of how Siberia was occupied by the Russians.

Down with Big Brother: The Fall of the Soviet Empire by Michael Dobbs. Alfred A. Knopf, New York, 1997. Vivid anecdotal history by a *Washington Post* correspondent who witnessed it firsthand.

Internet Addresses

BISNIS: Business Information Service of the Newly Independent States

> http://www.itaiep.doc/gov/bisnis/bisnis.html
> Run by the U.S. State Department, this web page is remarkably frank in its advice and analysis. A good place to begin the learning process. Features daily updates.

Russia Today

> http://www.russiatoday.com
> A quality news magazine updated daily. It includes excellent links to other sites and an archive that's fast, comprehensive and free.

Lonely Planet

> http://www.lonelyplanet.com/dest/eur
> Comprehensive information on Moscow and St. Petersburg as well as tidbits about the region.

CityNet

> http://www.citynet/countries/russia
> Contains good practical information on several Russian cities.

Yahoo Travel: Russia

> http://travel.yahoo.com/destinations/Europe/countries/Russia/
> A comprehensive travel site for travelers and those already in Russia. Includes a weather forecast, currency converter, and specific information for Moscow and St. Petersburg.